Original title:
Tawny Lights Among the Witch Dust

Author: Sebastian Sarapuu
ISBN HARDBACK: 978-1-80563-002-9
ISBN PAPERBACK: 978-1-80564-523-8

Glimmers of Enigma in Twilight's Grip

In twilight's grasp, the shadows blend,
Where whispers dance and secrets wend.
The stars awake with timid gleam,
As night unfolds its silent dream.

A flicker here, a shimmer there,
Mysteries linger in the air.
The moonlight weaves a silver thread,
Through tangled woods, where few have tread.

Beneath the boughs, soft echoes play,
As magic stirs the night to sway.
Each rustling leaf, a tale untold,
In shadows deep, the truth unfolds.

With every step, a breath is caught,
In glimmers of enigma sought.
The night conceals, yet reveals too,
A world where dreams and wonder grew.

And as the dawn begins to break,
The secrets fade, but hearts will ache.
For twilight's grip, a fleeting kiss,
Leaves whispers of a deeper bliss.

Sculpts of Light within Nature's Grasp

In morning's light, the world awakes,
As sunbeams dance on silver lakes.
Each droplet sparkles, pure and bright,
A sculpt of light in nature's sight.

The flowers bloom with colors bold,
Their petals weave stories told.
With gentle grace, they bend and sway,
Inviting souls to pause and play.

A babbling brook, a song to share,
With melodies that fill the air.
Among the trees, where shadows blend,
The dance of light will never end.

Each breeze that whispers through the pines,
Brings tales of old, in soft designs.
As sun and earth in harmony,
Create a world of mystery.

And when the dusk begins to fall,
The colors fade, yet still enthrall.
For in the night, as stars ignite,
We hold the sculpts of endless light.

Mystical Beacons Through the Fog

In shadows deep where whispers roam,
The lanterns glow, a guiding home.
Each flicker speaks of tales untold,
In misty realms where dreams unfold.

The river sings of ancient lore,
With echoes soft, it begs for more.
A shimmer bright, a fleeting sight,
The beacons dance, embrace the night.

Through twilight hues, the secrets weave,
In every breath, they gently grieve.
For lost in time, the destinies,
Awake the echoes in the trees.

As starlit hints of magic's grace,
Join softly in the night's embrace.
With every twist that fate may take,
The fog reveals what hearts can wake.

Luminous Pathways in Enchanted Silence

Upon the path where spirits dwell,
A shimmering light begins to swell.
In whispered breaths, the night unfolds,
With stories wrapped in dreams of gold.

Through canopies where shadows play,
The moonlight weaves a silver sway.
Each step unveils a glimpse of fate,
In silence deep, our souls await.

With ivy curled around the trees,
The fairy whispers ride the breeze.
They speak of wonders, lost and found,
In the enchanted night's soft sound.

The stars alight with wishes bright,
As journey calls beneath the night.
With hope entwined in every gaze,
We follow paths of mystery's maze.

Golden Enigma in the Evening Mist

In twilight's hush, a tale begins,
With golden threads that pull from sins.
The evening mist, a shroud of dreams,
Hides secrets deep, or so it seems.

Through glades adorned in amber light,
The enigma dances, takes to flight.
With every whisper, shadows twine,
And weave the fabric of the divine.

As silhouettes of trees entwine,
The ancient magic starts to shine.
With every turn that fate imparts,
We trace the map etched in our hearts.

The echoes hum of ages past,
In swirls of mist, the die is cast.
With courage strong, we chase the glow,
Through golden patches, soft and slow.

Flickering Spirits Beneath the Boughs

Beneath the branches, stories sigh,
From flickering flames that dance and fly.
In the twilight's kiss, secrets churn,
With every flicker, we discern.

The spirits flicker, lost in time,
Their gentle whispers, a sacred rhyme.
Through every dream, the shadows roam,
Inviting souls to find their home.

As twilight weaves its gentle thread,
In curls of smoke, the past is wed.
With laughter soft like morning dew,
They beckon us to chase what's true.

From leafy veils where mysteries rest,
The echoes call, a heartfelt quest.
In boughs that sway with ancient grace,
We find ourselves in their embrace.

Threads of Magic in the Night

In shadows deep, where whispers dwell,
A tapestry of dreams does swell.
Each star entwined, a spell does weave,
In moonlit glow, we dare believe.

The night unfolds, a cloak of grace,
Enchanting hearts in timeless space.
With every breath, a secret's born,
In gentle hush, the veil is worn.

Through silver streams and winds that sigh,
Elixirs flow from night's own sky.
A flicker here, a glimmer there,
The magic dances through the air.

In twilight's clutch, the shadows blend,
Whispering tales that never end.
Through winding paths of silken light,
We wander lost in dreamer's night.

The threads of time begin to blur,
Our hearts align, emotions stir.
With every pulse, we find our fate,
In threads of magic, we await.

Bewitched Ember Trails at Twilight

In twilight's glow, the embers spark,
With whispered tales that light the dark.
A fleeting warmth, a heartbeat's call,
We tread the path where shadows fall.

The forest hums, a lullaby,
Beneath the veil of dusky sky.
Each step reveals a hidden lore,
In crisp, cool air, we long for more.

With every breath, the magic thrives,
In glowing trails, the spirit drives.
The world transformed with every glance,
In ember trails, we find our chance.

As night descends, the stars ignite,
Bewitched by dreams, our spirits light.
Through flickered paths of amber glow,
In twilight's grasp, our wishes grow.

To wander forth, the unknown calls,
In ember trails where wonder sprawls.
Bewitched we are, through night we chase,
As magic weaves its warm embrace.

Hidden Sparks on the Forest Floor

In leafy green where shadows lay,
Hidden sparks in disarray.
A whisper there, a flicker bright,
Amongst the dew, a soft delight.

The forest breathes, alive with charms,
Embracing all in nature's arms.
With every rustle, secrets tell,
Of hidden spells in leafy dell.

The crickets sing, a midnight tune,
While shadows sway beneath the moon.
A dance of light, both strange and fair,
In hidden sparks, we seek to share.

Amidst the roots where dreamers walk,
In spark-lit paths, we rise and talk.
The magic swirls, a fleeting thrill,
With each new step, the world stands still.

In whispers soft, we find our place,
With hidden sparks, a warm embrace.
The forest floor, a sacred lane,
Where sparks ignite, our hearts remain.

Glowing Spirits Through the Misty Thicket

Through misty thickets, spirits glide,
With glowing forms, they twist and bide.
In secret realms where moonlight drapes,
They dance through shadows, shifting shapes.

The air is thick with magic's breath,
As silence whispers tales of death.
Yet life endures in spectral skies,
In glowing spirits, no goodbyes.

Among the trees where secrets sigh,
In shimmering trails, the phantoms fly.
Their laughter floats on misty air,
A playful touch, a gentle dare.

As night unfolds, enchantments rise,
With every glance, the wonder ties.
Through darkened paths, the spirits sing,
In thickets deep, they take to wing.

Embraced by night, the world transforms,
In glowing lights, our spirit warms.
Through misty thickets, hand in hand,
We wander forth, a dreamer's land.

Gilded Shadows of the Night

In the hush, a whisper calls,
Moonlight dances on time's walls.
Silken dreams weave through the air,
Gilded shadows, secrets bare.

Stars ignite, a shimmering sea,
Each flicker holds a mystery.
Night's embrace, a cloak of grace,
Mystic realms in time and space.

Echoes soft, the owls take flight,
Guided by the silver light.
In the darkness, flames aglow,
Magic stirs, a timeless flow.

Whispers weave through ancient trees,
Carried on the midnight breeze.
As tales unfold, the spirits sigh,
In gilded shadows, dreams may fly.

Hearts alight with daring quest,
In the night, we find our rest.
With every heartbeat, shadows blend,
In the magic that will never end.

Ethereal Enchantment of the Fading Day

As twilight paints the sky with gold,
Whispers of enchantment unfold.
In the hush, the world stands still,
Voices linger on the hill.

Amber hues blend with the night,
Carrying stories, soft and bright.
Golden rays stretch, reach, and play,
Ethereal enchantments sway.

Crickets chirp a lullaby,
Underneath the blush of sky.
In this moment, dreams will stack,
As daylight fades, we won't look back.

The breeze sings of days gone by,
While shadows creep, the owls will fly.
Through the whispers, magic flows,
In the dusk where wonder grows.

Time drifts softly, a river's bend,
Poetry of night to lend.
With every heartbeat, dreams will stay,
Ethereal enchantment at the close of day.

Golden Veil Over the Witching Hills

Upon the hills, the shadows twine,
Beneath the veil of stars that shine.
Golden mists dance in the night,
Witching whispers take their flight.

Moonlit paths weave through the glade,
Secrets in the dark displayed.
Each rustle in the leaves a sign,
Of ancient magic, soft and fine.

Flickering lanterns guide the way,
Where sorcerers once dared to play.
Chants echo through the gentle breeze,
In twilight's grasp, the spirit frees.

Gathering dreams on silken strands,
In the soft touch of ghostly hands.
A tapestry of time entwined,
Golden veil, the heart is blind.

Mystic realms await our call,
Trust the shadows, heed the thrall.
For in the silence, magic spills,
Golden veil over the witching hills.

Glimpses of Sorcery in the Gloom

In the twilight, shadows stir,
A flicker in the quiet blur.
Glimpses of magic softly sway,
Sorcery found in shades of gray.

Beneath the branches, secrets dwell,
Whispers of an ancient spell.
Winding shadows, forms they weave,
In the dark, we dare believe.

Ancient stones with tales to tell,
Guard the dreams where magic fell.
Glimmers of light, a fleeting glance,
Awakening fate with a trance.

Fireflies dance, ignite the night,
With every flicker, pure delight.
In the gloom, a pulse of grace,
Sorcery shadows, hearts embrace.

So linger here, in magic's bloom,
Where echoes sing of fate and gloom.
For in the dark, we find our truth,
Glimpses of sorcery, fuel our youth.

Secrets of the Hearth Fire's Glow

In the quiet of the night, soft whispers gleam,
The hearth's warm embrace tells a cozy dream.
Where shadows dance with a flickering light,
Hearts are drawn close in this magical sight.

Crackle of wood, a rustic song,
In its tender warmth, all souls belong.
Secrets unfold in the crackling cheer,
With every spark, a memory dear.

Whispers of comfort in the glow divine,
Timeless stories through the ages align.
In this haven, the burdens grow small,
The fire's sweet glow is a blessing for all.

Whispering Woods of Golden Haze

In the woods where the sunlight weaves,
Golden haze drapes the swaying leaves.
A path unfolds beneath the sky,
Where laughter mingles with a soft sigh.

Whispers of secrets the branches hold,
Ancient tales of the brave and bold.
With every rustle, a harmony sweet,
The tranquil night hums a soothing beat.

Amidst the trees, where fairies play,
Magic glimmers in the amber sway.
A gentle breeze brings forth delight,
In the whispering woods, dreams take flight.

Night's Silhouette in Warm Ember Light

As night descends with a velvet guise,
Soft embers sparkle like starlit skies.
In the warmth of twilight's gentle sigh,
Silhouettes dance as the hours slip by.

The moon whispers secrets to the trees,
Under its gaze, the heart finds ease.
Each flicker tells of wishes unmade,
In heart's deep chamber, memories stayed.

With every crackle, a heartbeat's song,
In this warm glow, we all belong.
Night's embrace cradles the weary soul,
In ember light, we find ourselves whole.

Reflections of Enchantment in Twilight's Embrace

In twilight's embrace, where dreams take flight,
Reflections shimmer in the fading light.
A canvas painted with hues of gold,
Stories of wonder and magic unfold.

Gentle whispers drift on the breeze,
Carrying tales hidden in the trees.
Each moment glimmers, a treasure to find,
In the twilight's glow, our hearts unwind.

Magic lingers in shadows' caress,
Enchantment weaves through this soft recess.
With whispered secrets that twilight bestows,
The heart knows the way where the starlight flows.

Alchemical Gold in the Witching Hour

In the night when shadows weave,
A potion brews, the heart believes.
Gold spills forth from whispered dreams,
Crafting fate in silver streams.

A cauldron's sigh, a flickering flame,
Secrets whispered without a name.
Stars align in a dance so bold,
Transforming all into alchemical gold.

Mysteries bound in ancient lore,
A touch of magic, forevermore.
Fragments of worlds collide and spin,
Within the depths, the quest begins.

Moonbeams dance on the potion's edge,
Casting shadows that silently pledge.
Courage found in the witching hour,
Embracing spells with timeless power.

Beneath the cloak of softest night,
Alchemical gold reveals its light.
Boundless wonders the heart untold,
In the stillness, magic unfolds.

Radiance Between the Whispering Pines

In the grove where silence sings,
Radiance glows on ethereal wings.
Between the pines, the secrets swirl,
A hidden world, a mystic pearl.

Moonlit paths kissed by the breeze,
Carry tales through ancient trees.
Whispers echo, soft and clear,
Guiding hearts that venture near.

Starlight filters through needles high,
Painting dreams across the sky.
Nature's breath, a subtle sigh,
Breeds enchantment as time slips by.

The shimmering dew, a potion divine,
Crafts a tapestry, intertwine.
Beneath the branches, secrets abide,
A radiant world where shadows hide.

Across the night, the spirits sway,
Bathed in the glow, they softly play.
In this realm, the heart aligns,
Finding magic in whispered pines.

Secrets Illuminated by Moonlit Wisdom

A silvery glow spills on the ground,
Illuminating whispers abound.
Secrets wrapped in moonlit beams,
Awaken softly from timeless dreams.

Each star a guide in the midnight hush,
Where heartbeats race and the senses rush.
Wisdom flows like a river wide,
As shadows dance and secrets bide.

A gentle breeze carries tales untold,
Of magic lost and treasures bold.
In the embrace of the silent night,
Wisdom blooms in the softest light.

The moonlight, a lantern for wandering souls,
Illuminating paths to forgotten goals.
In its glow, all fears dissolve,
As dreams and truths begin to evolve.

When dawn arrives, the secrets fade,
Yet in the heart, their mark is made.
Forever cherished in the mind's prism,
Are secrets illuminated by moonlit wisdom.

Enchantment in the Warmth of Dusk

In the twilight where dreams take flight,
Enchantment brews in the fading light.
Colors meld in a painter's hand,
Creating realms, both soft and grand.

A gentle hum stirs the evening air,
Whispers of magic, a tender care.
The horizon cradles the sun's retreat,
In dusk's warm embrace, our hearts meet.

Twinkling stars begin their dance,
Inviting wishes, granting chance.
With every glance, the world transforms,
As dusk unravels its vivid charms.

The nightingale sings a lullaby sweet,
Guiding dreams on unseen feet.
With every note, enchantment flows,
In the warmth where true magic grows.

Weaving tales in twilight's glow,
In the heart, the embers grow.
Embracing night with souls unmasked,
In the warmth of dusk, enchantment basked.

Echoes of Sorcery in the Dusk

In shadows deep, the whispers play,
Where ancient spells in twilight sway.
A flicker of light, a fading breath,
The dance of magic after death.

Through tangled woods, the secrets hum,
As creatures stir, to the night they succumb.
Of potions brewed and wands aflame,
The echoes call, yet none feel shame.

Beneath the stars, old tales unite,
The dreams of sorcery, pure and bright.
In each soft sigh, a story weaves,
The heart of magic, never leaves.

By moonlit paths, the wanderers tread,
Each step a promise, where shadows spread.
A world unseen, where wishes grow,
In echoes of dusk, the secrets flow.

With every hour, enchantments rise,
In whispers soft as twilight skies.
The ancient arts, they softly sing,
In echoes of dusk, new wonders cling.

Mystical Figures in Gilded Glimmer

In the heart of night, they shimmer bright,
Figures of grace clothed in light.
With laughter soft and voices rare,
They spin their tales through the cool night air.

Gilded dreams on silken threads,
Woven through the hearts and heads.
Their presence calls, a siren's tune,
Beneath the watchful, silver moon.

With every glance, a truth reveals,
In magic's grip, the spirit heals.
The gentle sway of wand and hand,
A dance of fate, perfectly planned.

In enchanted glades where shadows play,
They guide the lost, show them the way.
With murmurs sweet, they softly glide,
Each mystical figure, magic's pride.

As dawn approaches, they fade away,
Left in the silence, where dreams lay.
Yet in our hearts, they linger still,
In gilded glimmers, they bend our will.

The Scent of Enchantment in the Air

Upon the breeze, a fragrance sweet,
A hint of magic, where dreamers meet.
With petals soft and whispers kind,
The scent of enchantment, pure and blind.

In gardens lush, the secrets bloom,
Each bud a promise, dispelling gloom.
Where fairies play and potions brew,
The air alive with a wondrous view.

Through twilight paths, the aromas swirl,
Inviting every heart to whirl.
With melodies soft, the night draws near,
In every breath, enchantment clear.

The fragrant herbs, the distant calls,
In every corner, magic sprawls.
A tapestry spun from earth and sky,
Invokes the dreamers, as they fly.

As evening falls, the stars appear,
The scent of wonder fills the sphere.
In every corner, stories loom,
In the scent of enchantment, hearts find room.

Soft Glows on Ancient Stones

On weathered stones, the whispers glow,
Of ancient truths the wind might know.
Each crack and crevice, a tale unfolds,
In soft pale light, the past retold.

With every dusk, the magic breathes,
A tapestry woven with fragile leaves.
Where echoes linger, shadows play,
On ancient stones, the night holds sway.

Through time-worn paths, the seekers roam,
In glowing hues, they find a home.
An aura surrounds, with secrets bright,
Guide them gently through the night.

The watchful moon casts silver beams,
Illuminating long-held dreams.
With every gleam, wisdom whispers,
On ancient stones, magic shimmers.

In quiet moments, the world stands still,
As soft glows dance with graceful will.
Through ancient lore, our spirits roam,
With soft glows bright, we find our home.

Enchanted Glow of Autumn Mists

In the woods where whispers tread,
Leaves like gold dance overhead.
Frosty breath of morning's sigh,
Nature's spell as time drifts by.

Amber hues in twilight's gleam,
Echoes of a fleeting dream.
Shadows stretch, and secrets blend,
Every turn, a new story penned.

Pine and oak in hues of fire,
Dancing softly, heart's desire.
In the mists, a lantern glows,
Guiding souls where magic flows.

Crispness wraps the air so tight,
Woven tightly in the night.
An enchanted lullaby sings,
From the earth, a soft wind brings.

Autumn's charm, a woven thread,
In every glance, where dreams are shed.
As twilight paints the skies so wide,
In these woods, we choose to hide.

Glow of Sorcery Beneath the Stars

In twilight's hush, a spark ignites,
Sorcery woven, starry nights.
Casting spells with every breath,
Dancing close to life and death.

Moonbeams mingle, secrets swirl,
In the night, the magic twirls.
Each twinkle holds a whispered charm,
Cradled softly, safe from harm.

Underneath the velvet sky,
Echoes linger, spirits sigh.
Golden threads stretch wide and far,
Connecting souls beneath the star.

A world alive with whispered dreams,
Flowing through while stardust beams.
In the glow, all fears dissolve,
Mysteries of the night evolve.

Beneath the stars, our hearts embrace,
Finding solace in this place.
Where magic breathes in every glow,
In the night, we come to know.

Ethereal Whispers of the Night Garden

In a garden deep, where shadows play,
Whispers of secrets drift away.
Moonlight dances on petals fair,
Calling forth dreams, lingering in air.

Stars alight in a velvet sky,
Echoes of nightbirds softly sigh.
Crickets hum a soothing tune,
While fireflies weave a silver rune.

In the hush, magic breathes alive,
Gentle breezes, the fairies thrive.
Each bloom, a guardian of the night,
Cradles wonders, hidden from sight.

Dewdrops glisten on emerald blades,
In this realm where enchantment wades.
Every rustle, a tale to tell,
In the night garden, all is well.

As dawn approaches, dreams take flight,
Fading slowly into the light.
Yet whispers linger, soft and sweet,
In the heart of night, where shadows meet.

Cerulean Flickers Beyond the Dawn

As dawn unfolds in hues of blue,
Cerulean dreams come into view.
The sky awakens, brushed with gold,
Stories of night waiting to be told.

Wings of the lark, a joyous sound,
Nature stirs, all life unbound.
Morning glories stretch and yawn,
Beneath the glow of a rising dawn.

Whispers of wind through fields take flight,
Painted petals bask in light.
Each flicker a band of joyful cheer,
As the sun breaks, casting away fear.

Crisp air dances with tales untold,
In colors bright, the world enfolds.
With every heartbeat, magic flows,
In gardens where adventure grows.

Time drifts gently, sweet and slow,
Cerulean waves in the morning glow.
Under the sun, hearts intertwine,
In the beauty of day, all is divine.

Secrets Shimmering in the Thicket's Heart

In the thicket's heart, shadows entwine,
Secrets shimmer like stars that shine.
Whispers weave through the tangled leaves,
Guarding the tales that the forest believes.

Rustling underfoot as creatures tread,
Ancient echoes of the earth's thread.
A fox slips by, eyes bright and aware,
Each moment a dance in the cool, crisp air.

Moss cloaks the ground, a velvet bed,
Where wishes are granted and dreams are fed.
In the hush of twilight, magic is spun,
In every dark corner, adventures begun.

The oak stands tall, a keeper of lore,
Whispering secrets from ages of yore.
Each branch a witness to stories profound,
In the thicket's embrace, enchantment is found.

As dusk descends, the world holds its breath,
The thicket hums with life, even in death.
For within every shadow, a light shall prevail,
In the heart of the wild, where dreams set sail.

Glows of Mystique in the Underbrush

Amidst the underbrush, a soft glow thrives,
Mystique beckons where the shadow dives.
Sibilant whispers wrap around the night,
Luring wanderers with their magical light.

Ferns unfurl, cloaked in silver sheen,
Their secrets hidden, yet softly seen.
Tiny creatures dance on a breeze,
In a world where time slows, hearts find ease.

Moonbeams filter through the twining vines,
Casting a spell where the enchantment aligns.
Lost in the depths, where secrets confide,
In the glow of the night, fears subside.

The air is thick with a fragrant plea,
Inviting those daring enough to see.
With every flicker, a promise of dreams,
In the underbrush, nothing is as it seems.

As the night wanes, the magic shall fade,
Yet echoes remain, adventures laid.
Glows of mystique, forever they bind,
In the fabric of night, where wonders unwind.

Enshrouded Light in the Heart of Shadows

In whispers soft, the shadows play,
As moonlight weaves through night's ballet.
A heartbeat echoes in the dark,
Where secrets stir, and embers spark.

Flickering hopes on timeworn ground,
In ancient woods where dreams are found.
The silence speaks, a gentle guide,
To realms of magic, wild and wide.

Beneath the boughs, the mysteries sleep,
Awakened only for those who peep.
A shroud of night, a veil so thin,
Shall lead the brave to what's within.

Each breath a brush of fate's fine line,
Connecting hearts like threads of twine.
A flicker glows in darkest flight,
Enshrouded light dispels the night.

So tread with care, dear soul so bright,
Embrace the shadows, seek the light.
For in a world both fey and fair,
The heart of shadows holds its share.

Shimmers of Spells in the Candle's Flicker

In twilight's hush, the candles glow,
Casting tales of long ago.
Softly swirling, secrets rise,
In flickered dance, dreams mesmerize.

With every wick that bends and bends,
A whispered spell, as silence sends.
A glimmer here, a shimmer there,
In shadows deep, enchantments flare.

A tremble in the quiet night,
Where magic stirs, just out of sight.
The flicker shapes a silent tune,
Beneath the watchful eye of moon.

Each flame a wish, a hope unraveled,
In dusky corners, histories traveled.
The air is thick with timeless schemes,
Awakening the weaver's dreams.

So linger long in candle's light,
For shimmers speak of magic's might.
A luminous tale of love and strife,
In flickering flames, there's hidden life.

The Call of the Elders in the Evening Glow

As sunset bleeds on horizon's sweep,
The Elder's voices weave and creep.
In twilight's breath, their echoes blend,
With stories shared, from start to end.

In whispered tones, they beckon near,
Their ancient wisdom, crystal clear.
In evening's glow, their spirits roam,
Guiding lost hearts safely home.

A grove alive with tales untold,
Rich with the warmth of days of old.
Each rustling leaf, a message sent,
To embrace the dusk, in wonder bent.

The call transcends the ticking clock,
With every pulse, the past unlocks.
In sacred space, their shadows thrive,
Where the essence of all dreams alive.

So heed the call, dear wandering soul,
In evening's hearth, find your own role.
For in the light where shadows play,
The call of Elders guides the way.

Enchanted Secrets Beneath the Amber Veil

Beneath the amber, muted light,
Magic lingers, soft and bright.
A hushed unveiling of the night,
Where secrets dwell, just out of sight.

In glimmers cast on whispered paths,
Old tales ignite the heart's warm bath.
With every glance, a thread unfolds,
Of mysteries wrapped in twilight's folds.

Each shadow dances, twirls and bends,
While fairy lights weave timeless trends.
In emerald woods where silence breathes,
The magic spins from ancient leaves.

So let the veil of amber sway,
And guide your heart to brighter days.
Embrace the secrets hidden close,
For life's enchantments, we ought to dose.

So wander forth, let wonder call,
Through amber light, heed the enthrall.
For under twilight's warm embrace,
Enchanted secrets find their place.

Afterglow of the Harvest Moon

The moon hangs low, a golden thread,
A tapestry woven where dreams are fed.
Fields sigh softly beneath her light,
Whispers of magic weave through the night.

Shadows dance with the flickering glow,
Illuminating paths where wildflowers grow.
Owls call softly, their secrets unfold,
In this serene magic, autumn feels bold.

Crickets sing songs of forgotten lore,
While starlit skies beckon us to explore.
The air, it shimmers, rich with the yield,
A harvest of wonders, the heart is revealed.

Frosted dew kisses the pumpkin's skin,
As laughter lingers where joy had been.
With every heartbeat, the night draws near,
Embracing the secrets that linger here.

In the afterglow where silence sings,
The memory of summer dances on wings.
As dreams drift softly on moonlit streams,
Awake in the stillness, we celebrate dreams.

Luminescence of Forgotten Spells

In the corners of shadows, whispers are cast,
Of ancient magics and spells from the past.
A flickering light held in a battered book,
The soul of enchantment in every nook.

Faded pages tell tales of delight,
Of unicorns dancing in the pale moonlight.
Words woven together, a sorcerer's art,
Awakening wonder in the reader's heart.

The glow of the lantern, a beacon of hope,
Guides those who wander, to deeper scope.
In secret gardens, where dreams intertwine,
The luminescence of wonder will surely shine.

Each incantation, a thread in the air,
Stirs memories forgotten, we long to share.
A flick of the wand and the past reappears,
In the light of the spells danced through the years.

Beneath the starlit sky, we ponder and dream,
Of the magic residing in every gleam.
For each whispered secret and soft, gentle swell,
Unveils the enchantment of forgotten spells.

Radiant Trails in the Woodland Mist

Through tangled branches and soft, leafy trails,
The forest holds secrets, in whispers prevails.
Veils of the morning with dew gently cling,
While the world awakens to the joy that they bring.

Sunlight breaks softly, a glow on the path,
As shadows retreat from the day's gentle wrath.
Fairies take flight from the bark of the trees,
Dancing on breezes that curl and tease.

The woodland is alive, each fluttered sound,
Echoes of laughter where magic is found.
A radiant vision where time takes a pause,
Each moment a snapshot of nature's own laws.

In the hush of the mist, old stories unfold,
Of legends and lore that the ancients have told.
Every rustle and sigh tells of happenings grand,
In the cradle of magic, both gentle and grand.

With each step we take, a connection appears,
Binding our hearts to these sylvan spheres.
In the radiant trails where the woodland calls,
We discover ourselves in nature's soft thralls.

Saffron Gleams Through Whispering Leaves

Saffron sunlight spills over hills,
Caught in the dance of a gentle breeze.
Whispers of nature, soft, yet so clear,
Drifting through leaves that beckon us near.

Amber hues paint the sky with delight,
As shadows retreat with the fall of night.
Each flicker of color, a story to tell,
Of moments when magic and wonder befell.

The rustle of branches sings sweetly and low,
A serenade sung where the river doth flow.
Beneath the grand oaks, in the dappled light,
We linger in reverie, hearts pure and bright.

Falling like feathers, the leaves spiral round,
Creating a carpet of gold on the ground.
In the warmth of the saffron, we shed our cares,
As laughter and joy weave through the air.

In this enchanted realm, where seasons collide,
We find ourselves lost in the simple abide.
Every breeze carries tales of the past,
In saffron gleams, may these moments last.

Sorcery Illuminated by Fireflies

In the woods where secrets hide,
Fireflies flicker, casting light.
Whispers of magic softly glide,
Starlit dreams take sudden flight.

Each glowing spark, a spell to weave,
In a night where wonders bloom.
Nature's dance, one will believe,
In this realm, there's no more gloom.

The air hums with ancient tone,
Echoing what hearts desire.
Amongst the trees, we are not alone,
Guided by the firefly's fire.

Beliefs entwined in sacred art,
Where every wish begins to soar.
A glowing map leads to the heart,
And opens wide the mystic door.

With every flicker, tales unfold,
Of wizards lost and time forgot.
The night reveals the brave and bold,
In dreams where every spark is caught.

Saffron Shadows Dance

Underneath the saffron skies,
Shadows twist in golden airs.
Figures dance with joyful sighs,
Weaving through the sunlight's flares.

Petals fall like whispered dreams,
Nature's hues in brilliant sway.
Softly born on evening's beams,
Twilight brings the end of day.

Beneath the boughs where echo sings,
News of love and fate entwined.
Every step like gentle wings,
In this waltz, our hearts aligned.

Time pauses, holding breaths so tight,
Lost in moments, lost in trance.
In saffron glow, we find our light,
Embracing tales in every glance.

So dance your dreams under the stars,
While shadows play and twilight glows.
In this world, our magic jars,
Where forever binds and grows.

Ember Whispers in the Grove

In the grove where embers gleam,
Soft whispers float on nighttime's breeze.
Fires flicker, urging dreams,
While stars dance above the trees.

Silent stories softly blend,
With the rustle of the leaves.
Time unravels, threads extend,
In the hush, the heart believes.

Embers spark like wishes made,
With every breath, the night ignites.
Misty tales in shadows fade,
As the world succumbs to nights.

In this grove, the past and new,
Whisper truths both bold and wise.
Moments cast in amber hue,
With each flicker, hope will rise.

So linger 'neath the starlit dome,
Let your heart be free, unfold.
In the grove, you're not alone,
For ember whispers tell of old.

Golden Glimmers in the Twilight

As twilight drapes its golden veil,
The world transforms in painted hues.
Glimmers shine like spoken tales,
Each moment holds a magic muse.

In the stillness, colors blend,
Crimson dreams and sapphire skies.
With whispers soft that never end,
Time itself learns how to rise.

The evening calls with gentle grace,
Inviting all to play their part.
In shadows cast, we find our place,
A canvas for the open heart.

Golden glimmers softly beam,
Lighting paths through dusk's embrace.
In every whisper, life's a dream,
Under twilight's warm embrace.

So step with me into the light,
Where secrets dance and wishes swim.
In the twilight's blissful sight,
Let your spirit's song begin.

Elixirs of Light in the Witching Hour

In shadows deep where secrets lie,
Elixirs brew beneath the sky.
Whispers dance in moonlit glow,
A magic lost, yet still we know.

With every drop, the night ignites,
Transforming dreams in silver lights.
A potion here, a spell to weave,
The magic calls, we must believe.

Around the cauldron, spirits swirl,
As ancient tales and fortunes unfurl.
In twilight's grasp, the veil is thin,
We summon forth what lies within.

Remember now, the gifts we take,
In silence hushed, the hearts awake.
For every choice, a path unfolds,
In elixirs bright, our fate is told.

Candlelit Echoes from the Underbrush

In the thickets where shadows creep,
Candlelit whispers in silence seep.
Echoes of laughter, soft and sweet,
Resound among the forest's beat.

Beneath the boughs, old stories breathe,
Of woodland creatures and dreams they weave.
With every step on emerald floor,
We tread the paths of folk lore's door.

The flicker of flame, a guiding light,
Through tangled vines, into the night.
In every rustle, a tale is spun,
Of days gone by and battles won.

Embers flicker while owls take flight,
A world alive in silvered night.
In candlelit echoes, we hear the call,
The magic whispers to one and all.

Veils of Gold Beneath the Starry Canopy

Veils of gold, where dreams unfold,
Beneath the stars, the night is bold.
There, in the stillness, whispers weave,
Tales of wonder we dare to believe.

The slumbering woods in twilight's embrace,
Cradle the secrets of time and space.
In every glimmer, the past takes flight,
A dance of shadows in the tender night.

With stardust trails, we journey far,
In the heart of darkness, we find our star.
A symphony played on the strings of fate,
In the quiet moment, we contemplate.

Each twinkle above, a memory bright,
Veils of gold in the soft twilight.
With every heartbeat, we echo a dream,
In the canopy's arms, we find our theme.

Unseen Forces in the Flicker of Dawn

As dawn awakens with softest grace,
Unseen forces begin to trace.
Misty tendrils curl and twist,
In the early light, we can't resist.

The world is hushed, a breath held tight,
Waiting for warmth to banish night.
In flickers of hope, the shadows sway,
A promise blooms with the break of day.

With golden rays, the fears are cast,
Painting the future, letting go of the past.
In every dawn, a whisper grows,
Of unseen forces that guide and compose.

The dance of light through branches streams,
Awakening, shimmering, our endless dreams.
In the dawn's embrace, we rise anew,
Believing in magic, in all that is true.

Whispering Leaves and Flickering Dreams

In twilight's hush where secrets dwell,
The leaves converse, a silent spell.
Each rustling whisper, a tale retold,
Of hidden magic, a world of gold.

Flickering dreams in shadows play,
A dance of spirits at close of day.
The moonbeams weave through branches fair,
Unraveling mysteries, floating in air.

The forest breathes with ancient grace,
A timeless rhythm, a sacred space.
Each step soft whispers, a gentle tease,
Among the sighs of the whispering leaves.

As starlight drapes the night in lace,
We wander deeper, quicken the pace.
With hearts alight, the spirit soars,
Amidst the magic that nature pours.

And in this realm where wonders gleam,
We find ourselves in a fleeting dream.
A journey bright, with paths unseen,
Upon the winds, our souls convene.

Harvest Moonlight and Enchantment's Veil

Beneath the harvest moon's soft glow,
Where shadows dance and secrets flow.
The fields of gold whisper in delight,
As dreams awaken in the night.

Enchantment's veil, a shimmering light,
Casts glimmers bright through the tranquil night.
A tapestry woven with starlit thread,
Guides weary wanderers, a gentle bed.

In the quietude, magic sings,
Feeding the heart with hopeful things.
The air is thick with stories told,
Of love and laughter, of courage bold.

So gather 'round, let your spirits soar,
In the moonlight's embrace, forevermore.
With every heartbeat, the world feels whole,
In the harvest's glow, we find our soul.

With echoes soft, the night unfolds,
Revealing wonders, treasures untold.
As dreams take flight, and visions sail,
We weave our fate in enchantment's veil.

Dusk's Radiance in the Hidden Glade

As dusk descends on the hidden glade,
Where light and shadow meet unafraid.
The trees stand tall, their arms outspread,
Embracing twilight, where stories tread.

A radiant hush blankets the scene,
With colors soft, a tranquil sheen.
The chirping crickets weave their song,
Inviting all who linger long.

In whispers low, the breezes spin,
Carrying tales of where we've been.
A sanctuary made of dreams so bright,
In dusk's embrace, we find our light.

The fireflies twinkle in playful chase,
Igniting magic in this sacred space.
With every flicker, a wish takes flight,
Illuminating paths into the night.

So gather close, feel the night's embrace,
As dusk's radiance fills this place.
In harmony, our spirits blend,
In the hidden glade, where dreams transcend.

Mystical Beams Through the Forest Canopy

In the heart of woods where sunlight streams,
Mystical beams weave through bright dreams.
A dance of light on emerald leaves,
Each ray a promise, the heart believes.

The forest whispers olden secrets,
In delicate shadows, where magic begets.
Under the arches of ancient trees,
We find our solace upon the breeze.

With every step, the echoes call,
Through tangled paths, we rise, we fall.
In this rich haven where fairies play,
We chase the twilight, come what may.

A symphony sung by nature's choir,
Tunes of the woodlands, never expire.
In the shafts of light, enchantments bloom,
Banishing shadows, dispelling gloom.

With hearts unbound, we wander free,
Embracing the magic that's meant to be.
In the mystical beams that guide our way,
We'll dance with fate till the close of day.

Glowing Altars of Forgotten Magics

In the twilight's gentle sigh,
Forgotten spells begin to rise.
Ghostly echoes softly sigh,
Whispers weave through ancient ties.

Chants of old in shadows dance,
Glowing runes in night's embrace.
Secrets held in every glance,
Magics lost in time and space.

Beneath the stars' soft silver glow,
Altar stones hold stories near.
Where dreams and memories intertwine,
They summon forth a flickered cheer.

The air is thick with tales untold,
Of brave hearts that dared to dream.
Their legacies in silence unfold,
Bathed in the moon's soft gleam.

So heed the call of the night,
And wander where the past awakes.
Through glowing altars, seek the light,
Where every charm and wonder makes.

Golden Threads Through the Whispering Woods

In the depths of emerald shade,
Golden threads wind through the trees.
Tales of wonder gently laid,
Carried forth on softest breeze.

Murmurs rise as shadows play,
Each leaf holds a story bright.
Through the woods, where night meets day,
Golden weavings catch the light.

Fingers tracing ancient bark,
Every knot remembers time.
Guided by the silver lark,
Dreamers find the path to climb.

In whispered songs of fading sun,
Hidden magic starts to bloom.
Wanderers rejoice, for they've won,
A dance within the forest's room.

So tread softly on this ground,
Where nature's heart beats slow and true.
With golden threads forever found,
A world awakens just for you.

Veiled Luminescence in the Haze

In the mist that curls and weaves,
Shimmers hide from prying eyes.
Veiled luminescence softly breathes,
A hidden realm where magic lies.

Moonlight drapes the dreams in veils,
Whispers swirl in ethereal grace.
From shadowed glens to moonlit trails,
Every step unveils a trace.

Figures dance in hazy glow,
Fleeting glimpses of forgotten fate.
As night unfolds its secret show,
Bewitching forms anticipate.

Veils engage in softest sighs,
Luring souls to share the chase.
With every flicker, laughter flies,
In a world so full of grace.

So dare to wander, brave the night,
Where veiled mysteries take their stand.
In luminescence, find your light,
And let wonder guide your hand.

Candlelight Shadows of the Dreamweaver

In the corners of twilight's hold,
Candlelight flickers, soft and warm.
Shadows dance as tales unfold,
Weaving dreams in every form.

The Dreamweaver spins her thread,
Softly stitching hopes and fears.
In every flicker, visions spread,
Carried forth on whispered years.

With a gentle touch, she crafts the night,
Embracing wishes brave and true.
In the glow, the heart takes flight,
As dreams ignite and joy ensues.

Amongst the fading light we find,
A world alive with changing schemes.
Candlelight shadows bind our minds,
To place we enter through our dreams.

So linger here, embrace the glow,
Let shadows guide you where you roam.
In candlelight, your spirit flows,
Discover magic, make it home.

Ethereal Flames in the Mystic Grove

In the grove where shadows dance,
Ethereal flames whisper a trance.
Trees sway to a silent song,
As night envelops, the magic throngs.

Moonbeams shimmer on leaves so high,
Casting spells in the starlit sky.
Each flicker tells tales untold,
Of forgotten dreams and secrets bold.

The nightingale sings of ancient lore,
Of love and loss forevermore.
In this haven where time stands still,
Hearts entwined with a gentle thrill.

Fireflies flicker, a dance of light,
Guiding lost souls through the night.
In the cradle of sorrows and hopes,
The mystic grove teaches us to cope.

A soft rustle in the cooling air,
An echo of laughter, sweet and rare.
Ethereal flames will fade, it's true,
But in our hearts, they'll burn anew.

Secrets Woven in Amber Threads

In the hush of twilight's glow,
Amber threads begin to flow.
Secrets hidden, softly spun,
Whispers of a day once done.

A spider weaves with patient grace,
Crafting stories in her space.
Each glimmer holds a piece of fate,
In patterns intricate, small yet great.

The boughs above nod in the breeze,
Guardians of the tales that tease.
Time stands still in this enchanted vale,
Where heartbeats merge with the ancient trail.

Through the woods, the echoes call,
Voices of those who walked tall.
Woven dreams in the threads of night,
Cast a spell in the fading light.

As dawn arrives with a gentle sigh,
The woven secrets start to fly.
Yet in the amber's tender gleam,
Lies a promise of each dream.

Enchanted Glades of Dusk's Embrace

In the glades where shadows blend,
Dusk wraps all like a gentle friend.
Whispers flutter on the breeze,
Carrying tales of ancient trees.

With twilight's cloak, the magic hums,
As nightfall's melody gently comes.
Stars peer down with a soft, bright gaze,
Igniting wonders in a smoky haze.

Moonlight drapes the earth in silver,
While creatures around softly quiver.
Every rustle, a story spun,
As day surrenders to night begun.

Delicate blooms, in darkness bloom,
Their fragrance offers a soft perfume.
In enchanted glades, dreams take flight,
Beneath the watchful eyes of night.

So linger here, where magic thrives,
In the heart of dusk, where beauty lives.
Embrace the shadows, let go of fear,
In the enchanted glades, magic is near.

Fables Carved in Flickering Lanterns

Beneath the boughs, the lanterns sway,
Carving fables in the twilight gray.
Each flicker shares a tale of yore,
Guiding wanderers to distant shore.

The glow enchants the curious heart,
A beacon of hope, a work of art.
With every light, a history shared,
In whispered words, dreams are bared.

Children gather in the golden hue,
Fables spawn amidst the dew.
Imaginations take to flight,
As shadows dance in the soft moonlight.

With laughter echoing through the trees,
Time drifts on a gentle breeze.
Each lantern a spark of life's embrace,
Fables carved in a sacred space.

As night deepens, the stories grow,
In flickering lights, wonders flow.
In the warmth of fables, we find our way,
Guided by dreamers, night turns to day.

Glimmering Secrets Among the Shadows

In the depths where whispers play,
Glimmers dance and shadows sway.
Forgotten tales in silence breathe,
Secrets wrapped in twilight's sheath.

Amidst the trees that softly sigh,
Mysteries weave as the night draws nigh.
Moonbeams spill a silver thread,
Binding fables of the dead.

Each flicker tells of love and dread,
Of promises made and words unsaid.
In every corner where night unfurls,
Lies a world of hidden pearls.

So tread with care, and heed the call,
For shadows whisper from the hall.
They weave their tales with silken grace,
In this enchanted, shadowed place.

Let your heart be bold and free,
Unlock the veil, and let it be.
As glimmering secrets find their way,
Through the shadows of yesterday.

Ethereal Glow of Dusk's Caress

In the hush of twilight's glow,
Where gentle breezes softly flow.
The world transforms, a painted scene,
In twilight's arms, a realm serene.

Golden hues and violet skies,
Whispers of dreams as daylight dies.
Nature sighs in a gentle breath,
Revealing life, and flirting with death.

Bells of dusk begin to chime,
Marking the end of daylight's rhyme.
Softly tread where night unfolds,
In twilight's tale of love retold.

A dance of fireflies in the dark,
Guided by dusk's enchanting spark.
Let whispers of the fading light,
Guide your path through the night.

Embrace the warmth of dusk's embrace,
Find the magic in this place.
For in each moment as shadows rise,
The ethereal glow, a sweet surprise.

Invocations in the Softening Light

As daylight wanes, a spell is cast,
In softening light, shadows dance fast.
Echoes linger, sweet and low,
Invocations in twilight's glow.

With each sigh, the stars awake,
Whispers weave as old dreams break.
The night wind carries tales of old,
In secrets shared, the heart grows bold.

From ancient trees to the moonlit ground,
Mysteries waiting to be found.
With gossamer threads of silver spun,
A tapestry of darkness begun.

So raise your voice, let the night hear,
Let your heart speak without fear.
For in the silence, magic's near,
In softening light, dreams appear.

Every moment holds a key,
To unlock the vast and free.
In twilight's whisper, hear the call,
Invocations weave through all.

Ghostly Flames Among the Nostalgic Leaves

Amidst the trees where echoes bloom,
Ghostly flames light up the gloom.
Whispers of fall in every breeze,
Nostalgic leaves dance with ease.

A tapestry of russet and gold,
Memories gather, stories told.
In every rustle, in every sigh,
Ghostly flames drift softly by.

The past unfolds in twilight's grasp,
Captured moments, life's sweet clasp.
Letting go as the leaves descend,
In each flutter, we meet an end.

Yet in their fall, a promise stays,
A chance to grow in new ways.
Ghostly flames, a warm embrace,
Among the leaves, we find our place.

Embrace the charm of fleeting time,
In every heartbeat, every rhyme.
For as the flames flicker and weave,
In ghostly light, we learn to believe.

Sorceress' Lanterns Illuminate the Veil

In shadows deep where whispers dwell,
The lanterns glow, casting their spell.
Each flicker hints at magic near,
An unseen world, both strange and clear.

A sorceress walks, her secrets bound,
With every step, soft echoes sound.
Her lanterns guide through night's embrace,
Illuminating time and space.

In tangled woods where spirits sigh,
The stars above like lanterns fly.
They weave a tale of dreams untold,
A flickering dance of fiery gold.

Through veils of mist and silken threads,
The magic whispers where hope spreads.
Ethereal light from ages past,
A glowing bond that holds us fast.

As dawn approaches, shadows fade,
The sorceress' craft, a bold crusade.
Her lanterns flicker, a final song,
A promise kept, the night not long.

Ethereal Sparks from the Dusty Past

In quiet halls where echoes dwell,
Dust particles dance and weave their spell.
Ethereal sparks in the candle's glow,
Whispering secrets only they know.

Time drifts like leaves upon the breeze,
Moments captured with elegant ease.
Memories rise from the shelves of dreams,
Shining like stars in the moonlit beams.

A tapestry rich, woven with care,
Threads of the past linger in the air.
With every spark that ignites the night,
Stories awaken, takes off in flight.

An ancient spell wrapped in a sigh,
Carried afar where the lost dreams lie.
With each shimmering breath, we recall,
The echoes of laughter, the rise and fall.

Among the stars, in twilight's embrace,
Ethereal sparks weave their soft lace.
Through spaces where shadows gently roam,
They light the way, leading us home.

Gold Dust and Dreaming Paths

On golden paths where the wishes lead,
Footsteps echo, planting a seed.
Gold dust flutters in the scented air,
A promise woven with gentle care.

Dreams unfurl like petals bright,
In the glow of the soft moonlight.
Whispers beckon from the flowing stream,
To follow the thread of a perfect dream.

Each golden grain reflects the dawn,
A map of hopes that carry on.
With every turn and winding way,
New stories rise to greet the day.

Through fields of wonder and valleys deep,
Where wishes wander and seekers weep.
Gold dust sparkles in the fading light,
Guiding our hearts through the endless night.

With every step, the journey unfolds,
A treasure trove of stories told.
Gold dust glimmers, lighting the dark,
As we wander forth, igniting the spark.

Celestial Light Beneath the Canopy

Beneath the leaves where shadows play,
Celestial light finds its way.
Moonbeams dance on the forest floor,
A whispered promise, forevermore.

The canopy weaves a twilight shroud,
Where magic lives, both still and loud.
Each beam of silver, a guiding thread,
Illuminates paths where nightbirds tread.

Stars peek down through the leafy veil,
Sharing secrets that never pale.
Their glow inspires the hearts that dream,
In tranquil spots where silence gleams.

With every breath, the world reveals,
The ancient tales the night conceals.
Celestial light, a gentle guide,
In nature's arms, we seek, abide.

As dawn approaches, the magic fades,
Yet in our hearts, the wonder stays.
Beneath the canopy, forever bright,
We cherish the gift of the night's light.

Flickers of Magic in the Evening Air

In twilight's hush, the shadows play,
Soft whispers weave a spellbound fray.
Glimmers dance on the leaves of trees,
As secrets float upon the breeze.

A wand held high, the stars ignite,
Each flicker speaks of ancient night.
Beneath the sky, where dreams take flight,
The magic hums, a pure delight.

The moonlight casts its silver glow,
On hidden paths only few may know.
Unraveled tales of olden lore,
Awaken here, forevermore.

In this realm where wishes dwell,
A tapestry of tales to tell.
With every spark, a story starts,
And weaves together curious hearts.

So linger long, let spirits soar,
In flickers bright, seek wisdom's door.
For every glance at evening's veil,
Reveals the truth in magic's trail.

Glowing Secrets Hidden in the Twilight

In twilight's grasp, the stars unfold,
Whispers dance, their tales of old.
Secrets twine in shadows cast,
A glimpse of futures mingled with past.

The air is thick with untold lore,
As twilight speaks of magic's core.
A gentle sigh through the rustling leaves,
Hints at wonders the night conceives.

A lantern glows in distant sight,
Guiding lost souls through the night.
Each flicker reveals what eyes can't see,
Hidden treasures of mystery.

In every corner, magic thrums,
Soft melodies, the night hums.
With open hearts, let shadows lead,
To glowing secrets that souls may need.

For in this time when dusk bestows,
A world where only magic grows,
Keep your heart open, your spirit bright,
And dance with dreams in the fading light.

Phantoms of the Night's Embrace

In moonlit hours, phantoms weave,
Stories spun for those who believe.
With each breath, a chill may roam,
In the night where shadows call home.

Whispers of fate linger near,
As time suspends, and all is clear.
From darkened corners, voices sway,
Enticing hearts to drift away.

The haunt of dreams in silver streams,
Guides wandering souls through wild themes.
In this embrace, both safe and rare,
Love finds a way through ghosts that dare.

Yet fear not, for these spirits seek,
To share the magic, gentle and sleek.
In every shadow, a tale adrift,
Of memories lost, a precious gift.

So listen close, let phantoms sing,
For in their song, true magic springs.
With open arms, let wonder reign,
In the night's embrace, no soul's in vain.

Enshrouded Paths of Glowing Dust

Through paths enshrouded, dreams are spun,
Where glowing dust meets the rising sun.
With every step, the earth shall hum,
As mysteries beckon, softly come.

A trail of light for those who seek,
A journey whispered, bold and meek.
In every grain of sparkled sand,
Lies a truth, both vast and grand.

Wanders lost in the twilight haze,
Find solace in forgotten ways.
As glowing dust trails through the night,
It paints the world in soft delight.

With curious eyes, embrace the gleam,
Let go of doubt, believe the dream.
Each shimmer hints at tales untold,
In paths of magic fierce and bold.

So tread with care on this mystic ground,
Where secrets linger, yet to be found.
For in the dust of twilight's trust,
Awakens worlds that brightly lust.

Gilded Whispers in the Forest

In the heart of the woodlands, a secret does sing,
A tapestry woven where the shadows take wing.
Leaves shimmer like gold in the soft, dappled light,
Where whispers of magic make daydreams take flight.

The trees sway in rhythm, with stories to tell,
Of spirits that linger, casting their spell.
Each breeze is a promise of realms yet unseen,
In a world woven bright, full of wonder and sheen.

Moss carpets the ground, a lush emerald sea,
Where fairies are dancing, so wild and so free.
They twirl 'round the ferns, with laughter like chimes,
In the heart of the forest, lost in sweet rhymes.

Gilded whispers enchant, as shadows sway low,
In twilight's embrace, where the starlight will glow.
The night brings a hush, a soft sigh through the trees,
Where magic and nature entwine with the breeze.

Here in this haven, let wonder ignite,
In gilded whispers, where dreams take their flight.
For the forest is alive, with secrets to share,
A realm of enchantment, beyond compare.

Shadows Danced with Ember Glow

In the twilight's embrace, the shadows do sway,
With embers of light that flicker and play.
They dance through the night, in a jubilant tryst,
As stars peek above, like whispers of mist.

A grove filled with lanterns, aglow in the dark,
Where shadows and dreams leave a shimmering mark.
Each flicker, a story, each glow, a soft sigh,
As wonder ignites 'neath the vast, velvet sky.

The fireflies twinkle, a beckoning thread,
Drawing hearts closer, where magic is spread.
In the hush of the night, hear the soft, gentle flow,
As shadows danced boldly with ember's warm glow.

The night whispers secrets, so tenderly laced,
With visions of marvels, so fondly embraced.
Each flicker of light tells a tale yet untold,
In the spell of the shadows, the night's gentle hold.

As dawn starts to break, and shadows must flee,
The ember glow fades, yet remains in the tree.
A memory lingers, of magic and dreams,
In shadows that danced, beneath moonbeam's gleams.

Hazy Dreams Beneath the Moonveil

Beneath a moonveil, where whispers abide,
Hazy dreams wander, with secrets inside.
The night pulls you close in a silvery trance,
As shadows twirl lightly, inviting a dance.

The stars weave their light through the canopies high,
While dreams take their flight through the velvety sky.
With each gentle sigh of the soft, swaying trees,
The world dances lightly on a crisp, chilling breeze.

In twilight's embrace, where the magic unfurls,
Hazy dreams drift softly, adorned with bright pearls.
With laughter of fairies, and echoes of lore,
They beckon you closer, to glimpse evermore.

Each rustle, a promise, a flicker of fate,
Hazy dreams shimmer, as shadows await.
With the stars as your guide, wander ever so free,
Beneath the moonveil, where magic will be.

When dawn's gentle kiss bids the night to retreat,
The dreams will not vanish, but linger, discreet.
In the heart of the forest, where night meets the day,
Hazy dreams remain, forever at play.

Glimmers of Magic in Autumn's Breath

As autumn descends with a whisper so light,
The world is aglow in hues of pure delight.
Leaves pirouette down, in a soft swirling waltz,
With glimmers of magic, where wonder exalts.

The air is crisp-flecked, with whispers of gold,
In gardens of amber, where mysteries unfold.
Each breath of the wind tells a tale of the past,
As shadows grow longer, and daylight slips fast.

Crisp apples are ripe, nestled close to the boughs,
Where secrets of nature weave soft, tender vows.
Beneath every branch lies a story imbued,
In the heart of the harvest, where dreams are renewed.

Glimmers of magic, in every hue seen,
As the landscape transforms to a vivid, bright scene.
With each fleeting moment, the autumn leaves cry,
In colors that shimmer beneath the blue sky.

In the stillness of fall, where the earth takes its breath,
Magic lies waiting, ensconced in its depth.
With spirits of seasons, entwined in their tread,
Glimmers of magic, where stories are fed.

Cerulean Hues of Sorcery's Kiss

In twilight's breath, the magic swirls,
A cerulean hue as daylight unfurls.
Whispers of spells in the cool night air,
A sorcerer's kiss, enchanting and rare.

Stars scatter lightly, a shimmering shroud,
With secrets untold, beneath night's proud.
Galaxies dance in their silken embrace,
Where shadows of dreams meld with time and space.

Through meadows of wonder, where wishes take flight,
Each flicker of starlight ignites the night.
A tapestry woven with threads pure and bright,
Cerulean magic holds the world tight.

Beneath the vast sky, our spirits collide,
In the gentle caress of the unseen tide.
Crystals of hope gleam in silence nearby,
Serenading the heart with a soft lullaby.

With every heartbeat, the cosmos aligns,
In rituals painted with ethereal signs.
The kiss of enchantment, a timeless refrain,
In cerulean hues, love's essence will reign.

Crimson Shadows Weaving Through the Mist

In the shroud of the dusk, where whispers do dwell,
Crimson shadows weave their soft-spoken spell.
They dance through the fog, a haunting ballet,
As night casts its veil over dreams that delay.

The moonlight flickers, a candle in guise,
While secrets are stitched 'neath the cavernous skies.
With echoes of laughter, they glide and they sway,
Each heartbeat a tale in the shadows' display.

A tapestry rich, full of stories untold,
Of hopes wrapped in silk, and of hearts brave and bold.
Crimson whispers beckon with promises sweet,
As time gently dances with every heart's beat.

Through labyrinths twisted where paths intertwine,
The shadows embrace in a waltz so divine.
They swirl through the mists, with intentions unclear,
Yet a shimmer of magic lingers quite near.

In depths of the night, where reality bends,
Crimson shadows beckon as old dreams make amends.
So follow their trail, let the journey unfold,
Where wonder awaits, and the stories are bold.

Shimmering Charms Beneath the Ancient Oaks

Beneath ancient oaks, where the stars softly tread,
Shimmering charms glisten in whispers of red.
They twinkle like fireflies, dotting the ground,
Enchantments and secrets in silence abound.

With branches that sway, like thoughts in the breeze,
They cradle the moonlight with graceful unease.
Each charm tells a tale of the dreams we once spun,
A dance with the shadows, two hearts beat as one.

The leaves rustle softly, a melody sweet,
Inviting the night to the sound of our feet.
Where laughter and magic in harmony blend,
In the heart of the forest, all journeys transcend.

The whispers grow louder, with charms cast alight,
Beneath the great oaks, we share in the night.
Each shimmering token, a promise to keep,
In the depths of the woods, where old magic sleeps.

So linger a while, let your spirit take flight,
Underneath the great oaks, enchantments ignite.
With shimmering charms, let your heart find its way,
In the cradle of night, where forever shall stay.

Luminous Secrets Dancing on the Breeze

In the hush of the night, where the whispers are light,
Luminous secrets ascend, taking flight.
They twirl with the stars, in a dreamy embrace,
A dance of the unseen in shimmering grace.

On the breeze, they flutter, like dreams made of gold,
With tales of adventure and wishes retold.
Each flicker a promise, as hearts softly swing,
In a symphony woven with shadows in spring.

Beneath moonlit arches, the magic ignites,
As secrets entwine in the softest of nights.
They weave through the air, with a mystical cheer,
An invitation to dream, to love without fear.

In twilight's embrace, where all things unite,
The luminous whispers invite us to flight.
A journey through starfields, a map of the soul,
With secrets that shimmer, they make the heart whole.

So let yourself go, let the music be free,
Dance among the secrets, just you and the sea.
For in luminous echoes, our spirits entwine,
A journey of wonder, where magic will shine.

Hallowed Glow on Enchanted Paths

In twilight's grip the shadows dance,
Upon the paths where moonbeams prance.
Whispers of magic linger near,
Awakening dreams that shimmer here.

The leaves weave tales of ancient lore,
As starlit winds by softly soar.
Each step taken, a secret untold,
In hallowed glow, the brave and bold.

Beneath the boughs of wisdom old,
The heart finds courage to behold.
With each heartbeat, a spell is cast,
On enchanted trails where time is vast.

The night unveils a hidden light,
Guiding lost souls through the night.
Embrace the spark that flickers bright,
In sacred realms, where shadows bite.

So wander forth, oh spirit free,
Find your truth 'neath the ancient tree.
For in the glow of night's embrace,
You'll uncover your fated place.

Illumination of Starlit Spells

In the silence of a starlit eve,
Magic swells, and dreams weave.
Incantations float through the air,
As secrets dance with gentle care.

Glimmers of light on velvet skies,
Phantom voices, ancient sighs.
Each star a wish, a thought, a prayer,
An illumination, beyond compare.

Upon the hills where shadows play,
The night reveals a hidden way.
Through corridors of whispered grace,
Spells awaken in this sacred space.

Unfold the map of shining fate,
Embrace the magic that won't wait.
In every heartbeat, a spell ignites,
Illuminating forgotten nights.

So let your spirit take its flight,
Throughout the realms of endless night.
For in this dance of mystic binds,
The starlit spells, you'll surely find.

Radiant Secrets of the Eldritch Wood

In forest depths where shadows play,
The Eldritch Wood calls night and day.
Radiant secrets, a slumbering throng,
Echo of magic that ancient songs.

The whispers weave through branches high,
Songs of the past, a gentle sigh.
Each moment captured in emerald glade,
Where memories of magic are lovingly laid.

With twilight's brush, the colors blend,
In hushed tones, the spirits send.
The dance of light on mossy ground,
Each step reveals what can be found.

As fables emerge from roots so deep,
The forest stirs from its quiet sleep.
With every glance, a secret unspools,
Unlocking the magic in nature's schools.

So wander forth, let your heart lead,
Through radiant realms, plant the seed.
In the Eldritch Wood, where wonders reside,
Discover the magic in every stride.

Shadowy Flicker of Forgotten Lore

Amidst the night, where shadows loom,
A flicker glows, dispelling gloom.
Forgotten lore on whispers ride,
In every corner, secrets hide.

Through misty paths and echoes lost,
The shadows speak; what is the cost?
Of tales untold that linger near,
In flickering light, they appear clear.

The echoes of time brush softly forth,
Revealing wonders of immense worth.
In every rustle of the leaves,
Lies the magic that the heart believes.

So gather close, oh curious kind,
Let the flicker of truth unwind.
Embrace the stories of yesteryear,
For in forgotten lore, we'll find our cheer.

As daybreak comes, shadows may flee,
But the flicker remains, wild and free.
Through every twilight, let dreams restore,
The shadowy flicker of forgotten lore.

9 781805 630029